Cataloging-in-Publication Data has been applied for and may be obtained from the Library of Congress.

ISBN: 978-0998072814

Books may be purchased online at http://lorigetz.com/techsavvyusersguide

Cover Design: Jason Williams of JW Graphics.

Interior Design: Cyber Education Consultants

Editor: Babette Fasolino in conjunction with Miller House

Creative Consultant: Miller House

1. Technology 2. Internet Safety 3. Digital Age 4. Teen Workbook

First Edition

Printed in United States

The TECH SAVVY User's Guide to the DIGITAL WORLD

by Lori Getz

Forward

The World Wide Web, it's a big place, with more than a trillion places to go and over three billion people there. That's the biggest community any of us will ever be a part of and parents don't always understand how YOU will navigate this space safely and responsibly.

Technology is like slang, you decide what's trending! It's why no matter how tech savvy your parents might be, you will ALWAYS know more about new apps, games, social media than they do! Did your mom discover TikTok and show it to you? Probably not!

That's terrifying for parents. In every other part of child rearing, the grown-ups know about things first and then they teach you. But that's not the case when it comes to texting, posting, sharing, gaming, creating and viewing. You end up setting the rules and the pace.

So that's why this book is for you! "The Tech Savvy User's Guide to the Digital World" is not the "Dos and Don'ts" of online use. It's a clear (and hopefully somewhat entertaining) explanation of privacy, sharing, drama, health and wellness in YOUR digital world.

Table of Contents

You're Here, You Might As Well Try

Okay, so someone got you to open this book. Maybe you were forced to read it or maybe, just maybe, you know there are things you don't know and want to understand...

No matter how you got here, I'm glad you're here now. Let's get one thing straight... you are probably thinking it's that "Internet Safety" book where I tell you things like:

* Don't put your name, address and phone number on the web!

* Never talk to online strangers!

* The Internet is a dangerous place!

While there is some truth to each of these statements it's utter nonsense to believe that this is what Internet safety is all about. And furthermore, if anyone was to tell me that by trying to hide my real identity online I will be safe...well...I'd stop reading or listening right then and there. Why? Because it's just not the world we live in!

I should start by telling you a little about ME. I am a grown-up. I am a mom, a teacher, I have lectured with Federal Law Enforcement and most importantly, I LOVE technology. Not just the concept of technology but everything I can do with it. I am a gamer, a texter, a social media user, a follower and a friend. I post, I share, I comment and like, I communicate, watch streaming video (occasionally I binge watch too), listen to music, access information and I SHOP online.

Technology makes my life better! It makes things easier and it even enhances my relationships with friends and family. Not to mention... it's a whole lot of fun! But, there are some things about technology that I understand that keep me out of trouble. **Knowledge is power**. Technology is not necessarily harmful or unsafe, but the way we use it can lead to problems (some small and some big) when we make poor or uninformed decisions. So this book... it's not about what NOT to do. Instead, this book is about HOW to use technology in a way that is safe and responsible. You may even learn a thing or two you didn't know before. And THAT my friends, is where the power will come from.

Let's start at the beginning...

The idea that you could even keep your name, address and phone number a secret from the World Wide Web is almost impossible. Websites like zillow.com, whitepages.com, peoplefinder.com and spokeo.com are all in the business of making your personal information available either for free or as little as $3.99 (which is less than you paid for the Minecraft app).

There are even websites that take it a step further and show maps to your house, the social media you use, who lives in the house with you, your parents' occupation, how much money they make, what political party they belong to and your family lifestyle!

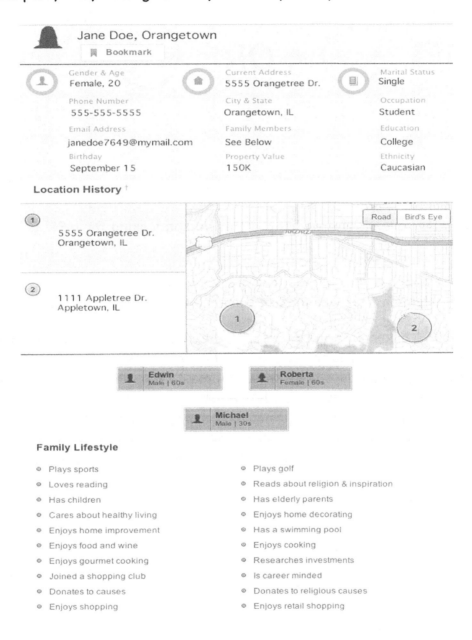

Most of the time, when we hear about these sites we think,

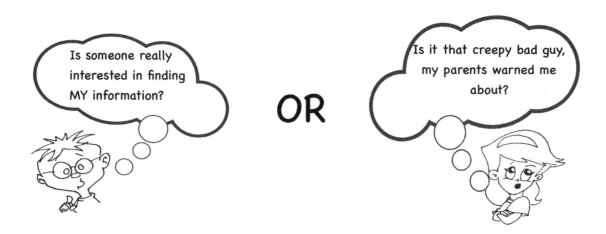

Is someone really interested in finding MY information?

OR

Is it that creepy bad guy, my parents warned me about?

Maybe... but the better questions are, "Why is this person looking for ME?" OR "How do they even know I exist?"

Internet safety isn't about trying to hide your personal information; it's about avoiding drawing the wrong kind of attention that would make someone want to get to know you better.

There are more than 3 billion Internet users and the number keeps growing. The truth is, if you are not waving your arms (figuratively) trying to capture the attention of a whole bunch of people, these stalkers and bad guys don't know you exist. But when you think the more followers you have, the more popular you are, well, that's when you become a target...not only from these "bad guys" but also identity thieves, frenemies, and people you thought you could trust but maybe you shouldn't have! It's time to get clear about what is safe, what is silly, and what's just senseless behavior when it comes to the amount of attention we seek and the people from whom we seek the attention!

Your New Digital Tattoo

Think of the Internet like a giant vortex that sucks information. It then takes that information and treats each bit of data like a piece of a puzzle. The result...your very own Digital Tattoo! Some people call it a Digital Footprint, but to me, a footprint can be easily wiped away. A tattoo is much more permanent and even if you try and get rid of it, there is always a shadow that remains.

Your Digital Tattoo is made up of the **accounts you create**, the **things you search**, the **games you play**, your **social media activity**, your **likes and comments**, the **pics and posts you share**, the **music you stream and download**, the **videos you watch**, the **apps you purchase**, the **places** Pokemon Go takes you and of course, **PUBLIC RECORDS** (birth certificate, address, phone number, etc. – pretty personal stuff if you ask me.)

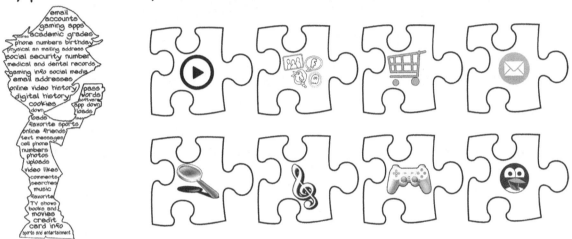

Remember that first account you ever created? Maybe it was Club Penguin, Webkins, Moshi Monsters, Fantage, or Animal Jam. You got to make up a screen name and even create an avatar. Well, that was the first piece of the puzzle.

Let me explain each piece of the puzzle a little more...

 Piece 1: When you created that first account, you had to create a screen name. It was probably a fake name because you were told that using your REAL name online wasn't safe. So you called yourself Tinkerbell, or SoccerStar or SK49T2. Whatever the name was, most systems require that you connect that screen name to an e-mail address, so they can send an email and verify who you are. That brings us to...

 Piece 2: Your e-mail address is usually attached to your first and last name and the city or town you live in, UNLESS you try to get very tricky and use fake information for all of that too. But it doesn't really matter because all of our devices (including cell phones) have a unique address called an IP address that is connected to your home address and thus your true identity. So now, just by creating an account, even with all kinds of fake information, the puzzle is still coming together to give you a full picture of who and where you are.

Piece 3: Then there's your searches. Even if you try to private browse or clear your history you are still seen and your searches are still collected.

Take a look at the Terms of Service before trying to go incognito.

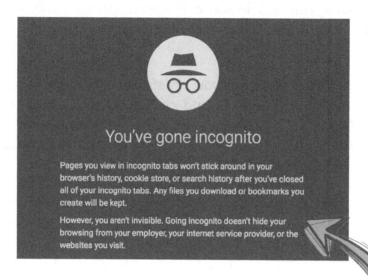

You've gone incognito

Pages you view in incognito tabs won't stick around in your browser's history, cookie store, or search history after you've closed all of your incognito tabs. Any files you download or bookmarks you create will be kept.

However, you aren't invisible. Going incognito doesn't hide your browsing from your employer, your internet service provider, or the websites you visit.

Do you see the part that says you are NOT invisible?

Have you ever noticed when you search something on a search engine, the exact item you want will automatically populate in the search field or an ad will appear for that exact item or something close the next time you log on? This is NOT a coincidence. Your Digital Tattoo helps create a unique experience that is meant for you.

 Pieces 4 & 5: Then you stream music or videos. Thus giving the vortex even more information about what you like. Next time you reach the end of streaming a YouTube video, pay attention to what happens next. The service presents you with other videos you DO want to see? Again, no coincidence, YouTube pays attention to what YOU like in order to make recommendations just for you.

 Piece 6: Purchases! Apps, music, books and anything you buy online comes with a price, and it costs more than money, it costs you some privacy too. The services are allowed to collect information about the things you buy and add that to your Digital Tattoo also.

 Piece 7: Gaming services use your location and sometimes even record your audio chats in order to learn more about you. Do you play a lot of FIFA or Pokemon Go? Have you noticed ads for other games you might want to play or even services in your area?

 Piece 8: Finally, there are the pictures, comments and likes you post on social media.

The Vortex collects each and every piece and puts it together like a giant puzzle that makes up YOUR Digital Tattoo!

Now at this point you are probably thinking:

These are great points, so let's explain that next!

First, it's not some creepy person sitting there reading through every message or looking at every picture (that has only happened a few times that I know of and those individuals were fired).

It's giant SUPER COMPUTERS that automatically scan every text, image, comment, like, post, blog, video, website, search, page view, etc. These super computers scan content for key words and even use a type of facial recognition software to scan photos and pull out key pieces of information. Let's say you take a selfie in front of a large chain store.

The service hosting the picture (e-mail provider, phone carrier, social media site, picture hosting site) has the right to scan that photo (using a type of facial recognition software) and the text (looking for key words) and pull out facts about what you like and where you are. THEN, they are allowed to match your accounts to stores and products that are similar to your posts.

Otherwise known as ADVERTISEMENTS.

So when we ask, "Who cares?" The answer is simple, COMPANIES care!

Companies want to know what you like and don't like, where you go, and what you do. Because if they can figure that out and send you advertisements for things you want, there is a greater chance you will click on that ad and therefore, the company will make money.

Hi, I'm **Joani**. Last year I wanted to buy a new car. I wanted a 7-passenger vehicle with captain seats. I went to the local Auto Mall several times to look at the Honda Pilot. I never searched it online but visited the actually brick and mortar store. Two weeks later I was at a hotel 80 miles from my home watching television online. A commercial came on for the Honda Pilot at the Auto Mall by my house!

How did this happen?

Well Joani it fairly simple. GPS from your phone identified frequent visits to a certain area. The vortex recognized a repeat location and sent advertisements your way.

At this point you may have some questions about safety. Here are some common questions I get...

> Are advertisers dangerous to my physical safety?

NO! It's not like someone from the company is going to show up at your door because you posted a picture of a hamburger.

> But, is this dangerous to our sense of privacy?

Sure! The more we drop into the vortex, the more information is collected about us and the larger our Digital Tattoos become.

> So does this mean we should all stop surfing the web, texting, gaming, shopping and sharing online?

NO! We just need to make better decisions about what we post, search, comment and share.

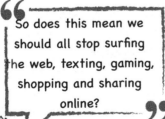

Privacy – The "Who Cares" Debate

There is another group that can see what we post, can you guess who? It's your Friends and Followers! So if companies can see what you're doing and your friends and followers can see what you are doing, are your posts actually private? I think in order to answer this question, we need to define the word "privacy." **PRIVACY means CONTROL.** Who sees what, who knows what, how much they see or how much they know. This definition is relevant both online and in real life.

In real life when we shut the bathroom door it's because we want control. We don't want anyone seeing us do our business while we are doing our business! Or when we say to a friend, "don't tell anyone but..." and then you tell them something private, you are trying to CONTROL how far the information goes.

Online, we need to think about how much control we have over our **texts, posts, tweets, blogs, snaps, share, comments, likes** and **views.** Has an adult ever questioned you as to WHY you shared or communicated something private online? Did YOU try to explain to that adult about private accounts? Did you tell the adult that it's a friend of a friend? Did you focus on the fact that there are billions of people out there doing the same thing and no one is going to come after you?

It's a common conversation and it requires some explanation.

Most of the time, when we share things online it's because we want a select group of people to see. Sometimes it's just a text between you and a friend, other times it's a video that captured some crazy new Parkour move you have mastered. No matter the content or where you choose to share, you have to understand that once you post, you give CONTROL to anyone who can see! That includes the COMPANIES and YOUR FRIENDS and FOLLOWERS.

Jaime, Piper, Charlene, Aiden, Roy, Lucy and I were in a group text together. Jamie decided she wanted to talk about Piper so we started a new thread without her. Half of the group began saying mean and hurtful things about Piper. Lauren decided to screen shot all of the text messages being exchanged and showed them to Piper. Whatever, I can't do anything about it.

Most online users don't care who sees what they have shared because they believe they are still in control. However, once you understand that you are transferring CONTROL of your thoughts, feelings, special moments and your image electronically, you are actually allowing someone to take that content and do what THEY want with it. Whether it's scanning it for information to add to your Digital Tattoo or screen-shotting a picture and redistributing or even opening something in front of another person, once you've relinquished control, you can't get it back.

You also need to think about who of those billions of people have access to your pictures. Have you attracted the attention of someone who might want to get to know you better? Have you posted something so controversial or upsetting that it goes viral for all the wrong reasons? Did you post an image that your friend's friend decided to share in another place and now your photos are circulating in places you never dreamed of?

When we focus on, "but it's on a PRIVATE account. No one can see it UNLESS I GIVE THEM PERMISSION" that's exactly my point! You choose who you give CONTROL and what type of information they can see, manipulate, repost, share or show others, turn into a meme, comment on with something nice or something nasty.

It's true stories like these that should remind us that you cannot control what your friends and followers do with your information once it is in their possession.

Section Review I

So, if "privacy" means "control", let's ask the same old questions in a new way. What type of information is worth giving up CONTROL?

Circle 👍 if it's okay to do 👎 or if it's something that doesn't belong being sent electronically.

Circle both if you think it's a good idea sometimes and maybe not others.

👍👎	Telling players what to do or which direction to move in a game?
👍👎	Telling players your favorite color or pet's name?
👍👎	Looking up information online to make you smarter?
👍👎	Responding to your parents when they text you, "Where are you?"
👍👎	A picture of a sunset?
👍👎	A Happy Birthday wish?
👍👎	A selfie while studying?
👍👎	A "Bad Hair Day" selfie?
👍👎	A dangerous trick on a skateboard?
👍👎	A text about someone else?
👍👎	Vacation photos?
👍👎	A picture of you and your friends having a great time?

Answers and Explanation:

👍	**Telling players what to do or which direction to move in a game?** No problem- as long as the trusted adult in the house knows you are communicating with players in an online game.
👎	**Telling players your favorite color or pet's name?** BAD IDEA- I know you have been taught not to give out your name, address and phone number online but your favorite color and pets' names may be the answers to your security questions and a good way to get your gaming account hacked! More on this later.
👍	**Looking up information online to make you smarter?** Sure! Information at your fingertips is one of the great benefits of technology. Just remember, what you look up will become part of your Digital Tattoo.
👍	**Responding to your parents when they text you, "Where are you?"** FOR SURE! Need I say more.
👍	**A picture of a sunset?** Sure, inspire others with your photography.
👍👎	**A Happy Birthday wish?** Not usually a problem UNLESS you are using social media and you are under the age of 13. Then that happy 11th birthday wish may get your underage friend kicked off social media.
👍👎	**A selfie while studying?** HMMMM....maybe. Are you distracted by the technology or just taking a break?
👍👎	**A "Bad Hair Day" selfie?** It depends. The thing about selfies is this... one selfie, great! Twenty selfies... no one cares anymore. If you are overdoing the selfie, your followers will soon get annoyed and start thinking of you like the kids that says, "do you like me , do you like me, do you like me?"
👍👎	**A dangerous trick on a skateboard?** Again, it depends. Is it worth breaking your arm for the attention?

	A text about someone else? CAREFUL! When you choose to give up control of your feelings about another person in writing, you can expect that it will eventually get back to them and you can't stop or deny it.
	Vacation photos? Fine to take (as long as you are enjoying your vacation and not just documenting it) but wait until you are home before you post them online. It's just not a good habit. It's like posting a giant sign on your house that there is no one home. Over the years we have seen websites like Pleaserobme.com (defunct now but had a big impact) that took your public vacation status and put it with a Google Earth map showing people how to get to your home while you are away.
	A picture of you and your friends having a great time? Great! Just be prepared for all of your followers who were NOT included to be hurt or upset. Maybe text it to the group rather than posting on social media.

*If anyone sends you a message, photo, or video via electronic means that make you uncomfortable, tell a trusted adult immediately. A **trusted adult** is an adult that makes you feel safe. Trusted adults may be your parents, safe helpers like policemen and firemen, a teacher or a family member or even a neighbor. It's a good idea to talk to your parents about who are the trusted adults in your life and then let those adults help you figure out the best course of action. No one has the right to say or do things that make you feel unsafe. So please, ask a trusted adult for help right away!*

When we create "private" accounts or send "private messages" we are choosing who controls our thoughts, our feelings, our special moments in times and even our images. We can't stop others from forwarding information, showing a picture on his or her device to someone else outside your following network. You can't stop someone from taking a screen shot or using another device to capture a photo.

So the next time you hear "It's private," I want you to ask yourself, "Is it really?" Is there any way this text, comment, picture, audio file or video could possibly be seen by someone outside the group and are you okay with that happening? Trust yourself and make your decisions about WHAT to post and with whom you share, understanding that you loose control.

Best Case, Worst Case, and Somewhere In-Between

Teenagers tend to make most decisions based on the "best-case scenario" and parents tend to want to point out the "worst case." I personally, try and make decisions based on the "most likely"...not to say that I don't think about the best and worst, I just choose to weigh all of my options and then make the best decision possible for me.

So let's say you have a couple of really good friends, Becky and Devorah. They recently started texting and using apps that let them exchange photos (that they think disappear after being seen by the recipient). Devorah sends a photo of herself making ridiculous faces to Becky just for fun. Now what?

If I was going to think through all of the scenarios, here's what it would look like:

Best Case Scenario	Most Likely Case Scenario	Worst Case Scenario
Becky likes the photo and sends back a photo of herself. She tells her friend, she is funny. Becky asks Devorah to make plans.	Becky takes a screen shot of the photo or uses another device or app to save the pic. Devorah waits – anxious about Becky's response. If it's really funny, Becky wants to show the picture to some friends so they can all enjoy the silly picture together.	Devorah has lost control of the image. Becky responds by telling her she's not funny! Becky captures the photo and posts it someplace else making fun of Devorah. Other kids see the photo and make fun of Devorah. Someone turns the photo into a horrible meme that goes viral.

This isn't an easy exercise and most of us don't want to take the time to make a chart with all the possible scenarios. Even more so, it's hard for you to make decisions based on the "most-likely" for a very good reason. Your brains are not fully developed.

I don't say this to be rude, I say it because it explains A LOT!

Have you ever done something... anything... and within moments you think to yourself "Why did I just do that?"

It's your brain not making all of the connections it needs to in order to apply reason, logic and impulse control.

As you enter puberty (don't worry- this is not a long conversation about puberty, I promise), there are several changes taking place. Everything from a change in hormones to your Limbic System (a complex set of brain structures, which is responsible for driving emotions), making strong connections. It's why you want to try out a new hair color, seek out a new group in Middle School and even try out new personalities. You are figuring out WHO you are and where you fit in, and it's all about how you feel!

Think of it this way, I love gummy bears, I would eat them for breakfast, lunch and dinner. When I was a teenager I would eat them ALL the time even though I would want to throw up at the end of the day. It's because I was making decisions based on what I wanted and not what I knew was good for me.

Then there's an overwhelming desire to be accepted by your peers. Peer-pressure is a real thing. It makes people join in with the group when they know they shouldn't, show off, and even be mean to others to look strong. You also have this other thing going on called "a desire for autonomy." You are ready to take on more responsibility and therefore obtain more privileges. In fact, most of the time, you believe it's your right!

As you get older, your frontal lobe connections in your brain become stronger. This is the part of the brain responsible for reason, logic and impulsive control (all the tools you need to balance out what you want and what you know is right for you).

Sorry Mom, my frontal lobe is under-developed

Now, the next time you get in trouble with your parents or teachers you can't say,

"Oh sorry, my frontal lobe is under-developed" but there is some truth to this. It takes a lot more effort to make good decisions at this age.

Now put it all together; the desire for more autonomy, peer-pressure, a developing limbic system, an underdeveloped frontal lobe, a surge in hormones that make everything go wonky, and access to a whole world with just a click or swipe and we have a recipe for trouble!

Technology allows us to do things fast. That means we can access information in seconds, but it also means we can make a horrible decision in those same seconds. When we spend a lot of time worrying about what others may think of us but spend only a millisecond before posting, tweeting, commenting, or sharing, you better have a strong sense of who you are, how you want others to see you, and how your actions will affect everyone else that may come into contact with that information.

Because I Said So!

Has your parent every said, "because I said so" when you asked for something? Does it drive you NUTS?

Of course it does, because that's not an answer. But let me tell you a little secret:

"Because I said so" can mean two things. Most of the time it means...

"Child, I know you want this but I know, as your parent, it's not the right time, place, activity, thing for you. But because your frontal lobe is under-developed and you are thinking with your limbic system, no matter what I say, you will not receive my answer well, so rather than going 'round and 'round on a topic you are not able to understand or accept, I will just end this conversation by saying, 'BECAUSE I SAID SO!'"

OR it means...

"I don't understand what it is you are asking! I'm scared. I am not sure what the 'right' answer is here. So I need some time to figure it out and in order to do that, I need to end this conversation and go look it up!"

17

You know a lot more about technology than your parents do and that can be scary for them. Sometimes it's up to you to teach your parents. If you think about it, technology and the NBT (next big thing) are very similar. You decide what's trending, not your parents. In every other realm your parents learn things first and then teach you with a slight bias based on their morals and values. But with technology, it's different. Who showed you TikTok first? Your friends or your parents? For most of you, it was your friends.

So the real question is, how do you make better decisions about the places you go and the people you interact with online so you can present your case in a way that makes sense to your digital immigrant parents? It will take patience on your part and honesty but, in the end, I have faith in your ability to explain the nuances of everything from Instagram to Pokemon GO!

But YouTube Pays Me Money!

Ah – the lure of fame, popularity and CASH! Yes, I know, when you create amazing videos and post them to YouTube it's all about the subscribers and page views. You get enough of them and YouTube will stick advertisers on your page and pay you money. Now even Amazon is getting into the game. I know a few YouTube stars myself, so I've seen this happen. But it's few and far between. So, for me, becoming "Famo," well, that falls into the Best Case Scenario column. We need to look at the whole picture.

You are an aspiring comedian.   You have your own YouTube channel with several videos that have gone viral.   You just hit 10,000 subscribers and some of your videos have over one million views.   Now what?

Let's take a look at all possible scenarios...

Best Case Scenario	Most Likely Case Scenario	Worst Case Scenario
Everyone loves what you post. You become famous. You make money.	You will be able to share really cool stuff with a lot of people. Your friends will feel the need to like ALL of your videos. You will post a lot and most of your followers won't care. You will begin to check your accounts more often looking for new likes, comments and subscribers. Your real friends will post nice comments and your frenemies will act like jerks. Eventually, someone will feel hurt or offended by something you say.	You will start to derive your self-worth from the number of likes and followers you obtain. You attract attention from identity thieves and they use your material to get information to hack your accounts. Predators are watching everything you say and do. Someone takes your videos and turns them into embarrassing mash-ups. You get a ton of HATE.

The things we say and do online always comes with attention. The word "attention" is not always a BAD WORD. Attention can be about someone listening to you, noticing an accomplishment, cheering for you out on the soccer field, or applauding after you sing in the talent show.

Negative attention is a totally different beast. It has to do with obtaining attention in the wrong way and from the wrong people. Over-sharing in order to get likes, or getting attention from the people who makes you uncomfortable are examples of negative attention.

I know a 5-year old who used to jump up and down saying, "Mommy, look at me! Look at me! Look at me! Watch me cartwheel, jump, fall..."

You get the point. And the mother responded with "NO!"

Okay, yes, it's me. I'm that mom.

I guess you may be thinking, "Wow Lori, that's rough!"

But I have good reason.

I want my kids to cartwheel and jump and draw and play and laugh and dance and just be silly because they enjoy those things. If I happen to notice... I will say something. But I don't want to have something SHOVED in my face and now my response isn't genuine.

Do you play a sport, or act, or dance, or sing, or draw, or paint? Think about this for a moment, WHY do you do these things? Most of the time we do things because we enjoy them. And there is NOTHING wrong with someone noticing you when you do something that makes you happy, feel good or helps someone else.

The problem is when we ONLY do things so other people will like the things we do or like us. How we feel about ourselves is the basis for a lot of the decisions we make. It guides choices about what we are willing to do for attention.

If you are an amazing and gifted artist, there is nothing wrong with sharing your gift with others in a gallery setting or online.

If you are a talented athlete, your gifts are shared as your fans watch and cheer for you.

If you are funny and enjoy making people laugh, as long as it's not at the expense of others (or disruptive to your teachers) continue making people laugh and feel good.

Share things that make you proud or excited, rather than soley sharing to seek validation.

So the next time, before you text, post, comment, share, etc. – ask yourself "what type of attention am I really looking for?"

When young people ONLY feel good about themselves when someone else likes their photo, or posts a positive comment, it is not healthy for your self-esteem. It's peer-esteem and can be dangerous to your well-being if it's the ONLY thing that makes you feel good about yourself.

> Hey, we're **James and Jordie** (brothers). Last summer we posted a photo on Instagram of that emoji everyone thinks is poop. Right under that, we posted a picture of our family on vacation just to see which one got more likes. Guess what? They got the SAME number of likes. I think our friends just scroll through all of our pics and just like everything. Whatevs!

It's important to focus on what makes YOU feel good about YOURSELF and relish the attention you receive when you didn't go seeking it out ...then you know it's for real!

We also need to be aware of the fine line between SHARING and BRAGGING. The difference lies in your intention and your audience. Imagine you saw the following posts on Instagram or SnapStory. What would you think? Are these statements BRAGS or SHARES?

There really is no right answer here. It depends on how the audience perceives the message as much as it has to do with the sender's intention. Would it be different if you send the same message to your best friend via text or posting it to the masses? Sure!

Posters don't always realize how others perceive their statements. While one friend may be incredibly excited about your concert tickets or new shoes, another follower may see it as bragging! It's important to think about your intentions AND your audience when you choose what to post. Even posts that are meant to be "shares" can cause a whole lot of drama when your audience misunderstands it.

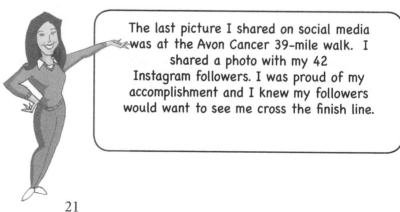

The last picture I shared on social media was at the Avon Cancer 39-mile walk. I shared a photo with my 42 Instagram followers. I was proud of my accomplishment and I knew my followers would want to see me cross the finish line.

21

Review Section II

Explain the difference between healthy attention and unhealthy attention.

Why do you think people BUY followers/subscribers? Is this a good idea? Why or why not?

Where Do Parents Fit In? How can you engage your parents so they better understand what's appropriate to share on Social Media, Texting, Youtube, TikTok, etc.?

Think about the best way to share information. Do you send to just a few individuals via Direct Message or Text (**DM/Text**) or do you share with **All Followers**?

Circle the answer you think would be best.

"I just won concert tickets to Flo Rida!"

DM/Text OR **All Followers**

"Happy birthday to me."

DM/Text OR **All Followers**

"Going to Maui on vaca. Later suckers."

DM/Text OR **All Followers**

"I got an "A" on my Algebra Test- WOOHOO!"

DM/Text OR **All Followers**

There is a law called COPPA which stands for the Child Online Privacy Protection Act that says online services may not collect personal information online from a child under 13 years of age. So that means you must be 13 or older to have any sort of social media account including Instagram, Snapchat, TikTok, Google Plus and any new social network that pops up after this book is published. While many people do not follow this law, it's something you should know! So be careful, that Happy Birthday message (to your friend turning 12) posted on the wall could get you and your friend kicked out of the network.

Strangers, Acquaintances, Friends, OH MY

When I say Stranger, you think what?

Right! Stranger Danger!

If I could abolish that phrase, I would! Because it doesn't give you the entire picture.

Not all strangers are dangerous and not all people who could harm you are strangers! PLUS, when it comes to our online relationships, everyone starts off as a stranger and for many teens those strangers quickly become thought of as friends!

There are good people in this world, and people with malicious intentions. And sometimes it's people you think you can trust that let you down in the biggest way.

A lot of times parents worry that the "stranger" you are playing with on Madden, NBA and FIFA, World of Warcraft, League of Legends, Call of Duty or any other multi-player games is some 50-year old bad guy who wants to hurt kids. And while unfortunately, that IS a possibility, there are also a lot of perfectly nice people who play too, MYSELF INCLUDED!

So how do you know the good from the bad? Unfortunately, you won't know until it is too late!

Rather than us constantly focusing on "Stranger Danger," we would ALL be better off if we focused on PERSONAL SAFETY with strangers, acquaintances, friends and family.

So there is good news and bad news when it comes to personal safety. Let's start with the bad news...

There are adults in this world who do not know how to have relationships with other adults so they would rather have them with children. So where do you think these individuals are hanging out? Where adults hang out or kids hang out online? Right, where there are kids! Why? Well, let's think of it like this...

Have you ever had a really bossy friend? They want to do everything his/her own way and when they can't make others do what they want they move on to someone else who is more easily controlled. Well, sometimes those bossy kids grow up into bossy adults and when they can't get other adults to do what they want, they look to control children.

It's important to understand that if anyone EVER makes you feel uncomfortable, online or in real life - that's the feeling in the pit of your stomach where you know something is wrong – that you tell a trusted adult immediately! It's not your fault and you did nothing to bring this on.

There is a process called "grooming" and some people are really good at it! Grooming[1] is befriending and establishing an emotional connection with a child to lower the child's self-consciousness and make them feel as though they can trust the person grooming the child. It's not just adults who groom children. I've even seen teenagers groom other teenagers!

But here's the good news, you can control and avoid being groomed with a combination of common sense and open communication!

Most kids tell me that they would NEVER go off with someone they met online. They would NEVER develop a relationship with a stranger like this. But let's look at the facts.

When you first meet someone they ARE a stranger to you, but as you get to know them and trust them, they stop being a stranger. So sometimes when you interact with someone multiple times online you start thinking of them more as a friend and less as a stranger, even if you've never met them face to face. That's why it's so important to focus on personal safety and NOT stranger danger!

Teens often avoid telling their parents about people they meet online for one of two reasons:

1. Teens are afraid parents will overreact and take away the account or the device.

2. Parents don't ask! They ask about your day at school, who you sat with at lunch and who you hung out with a recess or nutrition, but they don't always think to ask about the NOOB to your clan, glitching, or who "liked" your latest TikTok video.

But if we are going to focus on personal safety it requires open and honest communication and a little redefining.

Personal safety is taking precautions so that you keep your body, your information and your emotional well-being safe from being taken, exploited or harmed.

---

1   Wikipedia Contributors. "Child grooming." Wikipedia, the Free Encyclopedia. Wikimedia Foundation, 10 May 2016. Web. 12 May 2016. <https://en.wikipedia.org/wiki/Child_grooming>

The definition of a stranger is simple: It's anyone you don't know! Strangers can be male or female, young or old, good or bad.

Do you remember when you were little you were probably told, "Don't talk to strangers!" But then, Mom or Dad would take you to the grocery store and when the Grandma behind you in line mentioned how cute you were, your parent would nudge you and make you say, "Thank you" to a COMPLETE and TOTAL STRANGER! But wait, that goes against the rule of never talking to them.

> So, what are the rules about Strangers?

Rule #1 about strangers is simple, you don't interact with them unless a trusted adult knows about it and has given you permission to do so.

If you are allowed to walk into a store alone and interact with the store clerk, that is implied permission to talk to the strangers WORKING in the store. Your parents know where you are and have granted you such permission. You are allowed to do this because you have most likely demonstrated your ability to understand with whom you can interact and WHAT you can talk about.

You know better than to walk into the store and start talking to the clerk about your favorite movie and offer to exchange phone numbers so you can text later!

That brings us to **Rule #2** about strangers; you only give them information they need to know.

Can you think of a time where it would be okay to tell a complete and total stranger your name, address and phone number?

I can...

Ever ordered a pizza? You have to tell a total stranger on the phone your contact information and where you live. That's a lot to tell a stranger, but it's necessary AND you (hopefully) asked a trusted adult first if you could order the pizza.

> Hi, Can I get a cheese pizza please?

> Sure, what's your address?

Interacting with strangers online carries the same rules: the trusted adult (parents or guardian) has granted permission AND you only give strangers information they need to know.

We tend to turn online strangers into friends quickly! We complete missions together, have mutual friends, or seem to have a lot in common. But, just because you may know the same people or you shares common interests, DOESN'T make that person a true "friend." Most of the time it makes that person an "acquaintance." A person you kinda know. You may be part of the same group but not someone you would spend time with alone.

What are the personal safety rules for Acquaintances?

Rule #1; you don't engage unless a trusted adult knows about it and has given you permission to do so.

Rule #2: you only give them information they need to know.

Sound familiar? It should; they are the same rules we discussed when it comes to strangers.

When you visit your local grocery store, favorite restaurant, or coffee house, you probably see the same people working behind the counter. You KNOW these people are acquaintances. You recognize them, say hello, talk about the weather or your purchases; they may even know your first and possibly your last name.

But what about a "friend of a friend?" Is that an acquaintance?

a

Of course it is! They may know a little more about you as you may run in the same circles but he is STILL not true friend.

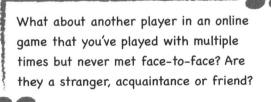

What about another player in an online game that you've played with multiple times but never met face-to-face? Are they a stranger, acquaintance or friend?

An acquaintance - definitely!

Let's test your understanding with a typical scenario:

You play Minecraft on a public multi-player server. You see another player who wants to join you as you build a Mayan Ruin for fun. You do not know each other in real life (IRL) but you have seen her work on the server before, you've even chatted a few times, not to mention she has a lot of tools, diamonds and gold to share. What do you do?

Best Case Scenario	Most Likely Scenario	Worst Case Scenario
You build the most amazing city ever. She spits diamonds at you and you get to keep them. You realize you have a lot in common and become great friends. You build an amazing city together and have fun doing it.	You will give away too much information to this person and wonder if they will use it against you. You start to believe this person is your friend and you wonder if you should tell your parents about it.	This player is a really bad person who is trying to get to know you better in order to trick you into meeting him/her IRL. This person convinces you to share your account password to help you get more tools and they hack your account and steal all of your tools. They figure out who you really are and impersonate you online making you look like a fool.

Unfortunately, all three of these worst-case scenarios have happened in real life. Not all the time, but it does happen.

The problem is when you meet people online through gaming, social media, or chat rooms you forget your real-life rules about strangers and acquaintances. You start to believe that the rules ONLINE are different. But that's just not true!

I'm **Dylan**. I'm a rising YouTube star because I'm crazy good at anime. A fellow YouTuber, named Animerator, reached out and complimented my work. He too is an anime creator. Animerator asked me about how I got started, my favorite type of anime, my inspirations, and my favorite color. I know not to share my personal information with anyone online, I never tell my real name, age, address or phone number. But these questions didn't seem like personal information to me so I answered! One day, I tried to log in to my account and found that my password was not recognized. I visited my channel and found that someone had taken down ALL of my videos! I was going to message Animerator about what happened and when I saw his page I found that he had stolen all of my videos and were claiming them as his OWN! How did this happen?

It was quite simple actually. Although Dylan may not have shared his PASSWORD with Animerator, he accidentally shared the answers to his security questions. Most of the time, we don't think about this but it's one of the ways hackers access accounts. They make you believe they are asking innocuous questions when really they are 'phishing' for information.

In this example Dylan used his love of anime to answer security questions because he knew he would remember the answers AND it would be difficult for others to guess. When the question was what is your favorite pet's name, Dylan used his favorite anime character as the answer. He was being SMART because he used a code to answer the questions but forgot about **Rule #2**: Never give anyone information they do not need to know.

I've seen the same thing happen time and time again in social media too! Teens often use fake names in social media to protect their identity but they forget that by talking about a best friend, favorite pet, or taking pictures in sport or school uniforms, it gives an identity thief all they need to know to hack your accounts and/or pretend to be you!

Your name, address, and phone number are just the tip of the iceberg when it comes to over-sharing. You also need to be thinking about things you freely give away that now others can control.

I'm **Jordie** and I have an Instagram account.
I **KNOW** the more followers I have, the more popular
I become. But my parents insist I use a private account
and only allow people to follow me that I know.
One day my parents' bank account was accessed by an
identity thief stealing over $2000. I couldn't imagine that
I had anything to do with it. But when the fraud
department investigated, this is what they found...

One of MY followers had hacked into their online banking
account. I was shocked! Let me explain how this
worked. It's a bit complicated so I will use a diagram.

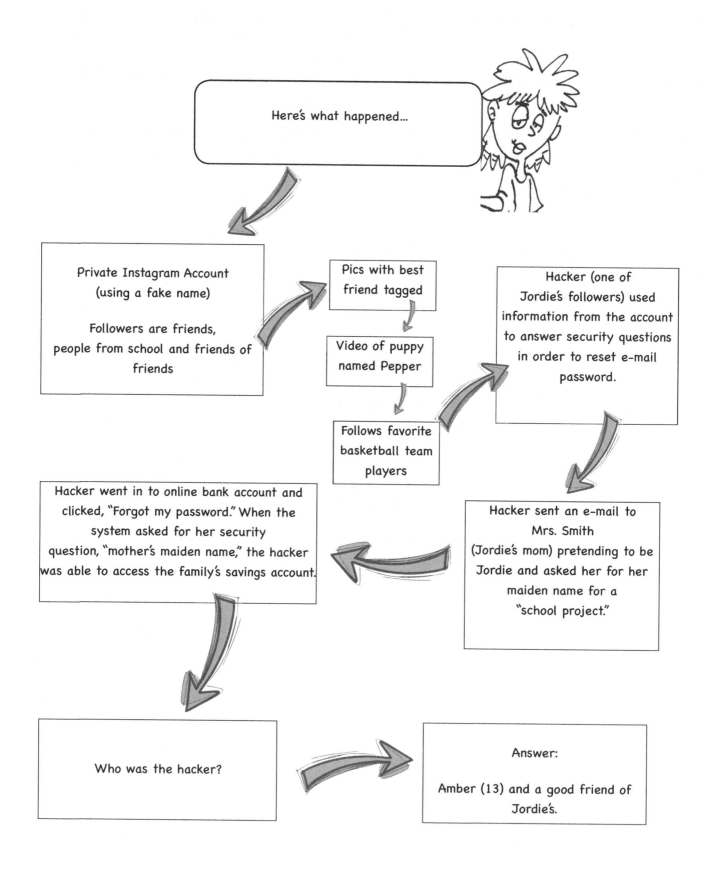

Here's what happened...

Private Instagram Account (using a fake name)

Followers are friends, people from school and friends of friends

Pics with best friend tagged

Video of puppy named Pepper

Follows favorite basketball team players

Hacker (one of Jordie's followers) used information from the account to answer security questions in order to reset e-mail password.

Hacker sent an e-mail to Mrs. Smith (Jordie's mom) pretending to be Jordie and asked her for her maiden name for a "school project."

Hacker went in to online bank account and clicked, "Forgot my password." When the system asked for her security question, "mother's maiden name," the hacker was able to access the family's savings account.

Who was the hacker?

Answer:

Amber (13) and a good friend of Jordie's.

Are you wondering why Amber hacked Jordie and his family's accounts?

I was too!

When the police arrested Amber she was in shock. To Amber, the whole thing was a joke. She just wanted to see how far she could take things. Not only did she steal from Jordie's family, but while she had access to his e-mail, she sent messages to his teachers (calling them disgusting names), to his friends (ruining relationships that had lasted years), and created accounts using Jordie's information that didn't portray him in the best light.

Amber is a usually a very nice person. She has never been known as a bully or a troublemaker. But as a curious 13-year old with an under-developed frontal lobe, she made a HUGE mistake! She never thought her joke would have such serious consequences.

Amber was prosecuted and pleaded guilty to harassment, impersonation, hacking, and theft. While she was not incarcerated she is currently on probation, must complete over 300 hours of community service and has lost all use of technology until her probation is complete.

This is an extreme case. Most of the time, when I become aware of a teen hacking situation, it revolves around creating digital drama! More on that later.

But how could a friend do this to another friend? It's hard to imagine that a friend could betray you like this. I'm not saying that you shouldn't trust anyone, I'm saying it's important to keep your personal safety in mind at all times. Think about what you post, where you post it, and with whom you are sharing: is it kind, is it honest and is it necessary?

So what makes someone a TRUE friend?

A true friend is someone you have known for a long time. And over time you have shared small pieces of information and set boundaries and this person respected your privacy and boundaries- thus building TRUST. Also, a true friend is someone your parents or guardians KNOW about!

At this point in your life your parents may not have met every person you consider to be a true friend, you may not have had them to your house but you see them every day at school. But you should at least TELL your parents about this person. Because if someone is important to you, then they should be important to your parents as well.

If your parents aren't asking about the friends/followers you have online, it's YOUR job to tell them about these people. If you are worried about your parents taking away the account or your device because you met someone online, then you already know you are doing something they won't be happy with.

I get it...you don't want your parents all up in your business all the time. But just take a minute to think about why? Is it because you want more independence? Is it because you are keeping someone's else's secret? Or is it because you don't want to be judged?

With independence comes with responsibility. Secrets come with stress. And no one wants to be judged! While I understand that as a parent, I would like you to know something important. Parents are usually on team "child" and NOT on team "trouble." Meaning, they want to be there for you. They just may need you to tell them HOW you want them to be there for you. So if you aren't sure if your friend is in trouble, talk to your trusted adult so they can help you decide what can be kept quiet and what needs additional intervention.

If you are keeping secrets for a friend that could be harmful to that person or if the secret may hurt someone else, you shouldn't carry the burden alone. Relationships that require hiding them from your parents are NOT healthy relationships. When it requires secrecy, there is something wrong!

Review Section III

What type of information is okay to share? How do you decide, and where do you share that information? Complete the table below.

(Remember, this goes way beyond just your name, address and phone number. Don't forget about what we discussed regarding Control and Attention.)

Location/Type of Communication	Strangers	Acquaintances	Friends
In an Online Game (FIFA, Madden, WOW, Fortnite)	Example: Which way to move, shoot, build, etc. Limited to the game.	Example: Which way to move, shoot, build, etc. Limited to the game.	Example: Which way to move, shoot, build, etc. Limited to the game. Even though they are friends, its still a public space and I don't know who else is lurking around.
Discussion board or public chat room			
Social Media			
Text or Direct Messages			

What personal safety rules will you follow when:

You encounter another player in a game that is not a true friend? What can you say or do with this person in the gaming environment?

```



```

What are the rules about following a celebrity or high profile person (even a presidential candidate)? Is a celebrity you have never met before, but maybe have seen ALL of his/her work; a stranger, acquaintance or friend? Circle the correct answer.

```



```

Who is your trusted adult? When you feel uncomfortable, with whom can you talk? Everyone needs this person in his or her life. Not everyone will choose his or her parent and that's okay as long as you have an adult you can turn to in a tough situation. You can have more than one.

```



```

I Did Not Want to See THAT!

We all feel differently about the things we see online. But, you can't unsee something once you've been exposed. We should all have the right to decide what we want to see and what we don't and it's not fair when other people, spammers or even tricky advertisers force-feed us images that we didn't want to see in the first place!

The Internet is a HUGE community with over one trillion websites and more than three billion people there. It's the biggest community you will ever be a part of. You have to understand that not every place online is meant for you nor is every conversation. There is some content online that could actually be harmful to you and your perception about real life relationships and actions. Not everything you see online is real or is representative of your family's values.

The average age someone is exposed to explicit material is 11-years old. Explicit material includes everything from crude language and violence to images of body parts that are normally covered by a bathing suit. Even though you might be curious, the Internet is not great place to go looking. "Why?" You might ask...

Well first, because if you don't know enough about what you are looking at you don't know if what you are seeing is accurate. Second, you may accidentally see something you just weren't ready to see!

Someone sent me a link and I had no idea what I was opening. It was kinda gross .- Hayden (7th grade)

Some content online depicts situations that are fake but may look real. It's important to understand that whether it's a violent act, or a portrayal of a grown-up relationship, not everything online is accurate!

Sometimes, when a young person is exposed to explicit content too early, their brain begins to play tricks on him/her and make him/her want to watch more and more (kind of like drugs). It can quickly become an obsession. If this is already happening to you, please don't be embarrassed. You have been sucked in and you may need some help getting on a better path. Talk to a trusted adult; there is no shame in asking for help.

If this chapter is making you curious about what I am talking about, please talk to your parents or guardian first before going online and trying to figure it out. Remember that everything you browse online, even if you clear your history or private browse, is not actually private. It will be thrown into the vortex as part of your Digital Tattoo and you may end up with advertisements that might shock you and your parents.

That's NOT Fair!

This phase is GROSSLY overused! Fair does not mean equal, it means everyone gets what they need.

So let's talk about how we make decisions about what is fair when it comes to screen time.

There is no magic number when it comes to the amount of screen time you should have each day. There are so many things you have to take into consideration to decide what is right for you on any particular day.

Hi, I'm **Joey**. I have a two-year old baby sister, we call her Nugget. Nugget and I both love to watch television. In the mornings before school, mom lets Nugget watch TV but not ME. It's so not fair!

Are you eating well? Getting plenty of exercise (at least an hour a day)? Going to bed at a reasonable hour (you need between 9.25 to 11 hours of sleep per night)? Do you spend time with friends and family face to face? How much time do you need for homework and chores? What activities, practices, games or rehearsals do you have to go to today? Can you stop playing, texting, watching when it's time to do something else?

You need a good hour before bed to disconnect and decompress. If you text up until the time you go to bed, you won't stop! You will constantly be waiting for the next reply. It's important to set a stopping time for yourself and let your friends know you are logging off now. That way your brain has time to relax and your body starts to get ready to sleep.

In order to figure out how much screen time is right for you each day, you must start with looking at all of the things you HAVE to do first. Take a look at the chart below:

If there are 24 hours in a day...

Get ready for school	1/2 hour
School	7 hours
Homework	1 1/2 hours
Dinner	1/2 hour
Chores	1/2 hour
After school activities and/or exercise	2 hours (including travel time)
Reading	1/2 hour
Ready for bed/shower	1/2 hour
Sleep	9 1/4 hours

= 22 1/4 hours

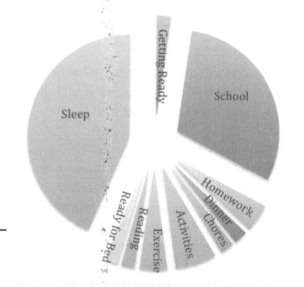

That only leaves one and 3/4 hours for down time and not all of that should be spent sitting in front of a screen.

Since your chart may not look exactly like mine, you should create your own in order to see how much time you really have during the week to get everything done. You may even be surprised!

Your whole body, including your brain, needs to be exercised every day in a variety of ways. It's important to keep well rounded and it's even important to be BORED sometimes!

Out of boredom comes creativity and innovation . It's a skill that requires practice. If you ONLY play video games or check SnapChat updates, you are missing out on a lot.

Think of something you enjoyed doing BEFORE you had access to a device. What was it? Why did you stop doing it? If you still do it, good for you! Has gaming or social media stopped you from your other passions or hobbies?

It's not that I am anti-gaming, anti-texting or anti-TV and videos. I am just all about balance.

If my family and I are going to watch a two-hour movie, then we will spend at least two hours doing something active.

What about this 2-hour per day rule my doctor told me about? Is that ALL the screen time I can have for the WHOLE DAY?

The two-hour per day recommendation came from an obesity study and not a technology study. Basically, we KNOW- the more you sit... the bigger you get! So if you are playing Wii and jumping all over the place, that isn't the same to me as sitting on the couch binge watching your favorite TV show. However, if you are in a place where you can go outside to play those same games, there is a huge benefit to the Vitamin D you get when you play outside. You can't get that health benefit from Wii Tennis.

The best rule of thumb for screen time is this:

1. You should move around more than you sit around! The more you sit, the bigger you get.

2. Take frequent breaks when using technology for a long period of time: writing papers, research, and even binge watching ;-). Repetitive motion (doing the same thing over and over again like gaming, texting, and typing) can cause stress and even damage to your hands, eyes, necks, backs or wrists. Get up, move around and stretch your body every 20 minutes.

3. Don't use technology when you should be doing something else! Trying to update statuses, commenting and liking a photo, or participating in a group text while doing homework or studying, is a terrible idea! We will talk about this in more detail in the next chapter.

4. Texting one person while having a face-to-face conversation with someone else is RUDE ! If

you need to take a call or respond to a text, excuse yourself, walk away, do what you need to do and then return to the face-to-face conversation.

5. Dinner time is a great time to enjoy the people around you. There is no reason to bring your friends via your cell phone or other device to the dinner table!

Some common questions I get on this topic:

What about on the weekends? Can I have ALL the screen time I want?

Look at the bigger picture on the weekends. Are you moving more than you are sitting around? Can you stop yourself after 20-30 minutes and do something else so you don't hurt your body? Have you used your creative and innovative side of your brain? Have you gotten plenty of sleep, vitamin D, etc.? Binge watching or video game marathons every once in a while is part of being a kid (hey, even adults like to do it too sometimes). But when it's out of balance and out of control you may need to take a look at whether or not you have a healthy balance.

If I have to do homework online does that count as my screen time for the whole day?

Homework is NOT the same as free time. Teachers structure homework and someone else sets expectations for you. Free time is user-centered; you get to decide what you do and how you do it. So in my opinion, homework screen time and free-time screen time are NOT the same.

But understanding obligations and living up to expectations are important. And right now, your JOB (or obligation) is school.

Should I get the same amount of screen time each day?

It's time to figure out how to do your JOB to the best of your ability. And if you are rushing through an English assignment so you can get your "screen-time" you are probably not doing a great job. And if you had to spend two hours writing a history paper in a particular day, you have sat for a LONG TIME and your fingers, hands, wrists, back and neck have been in the same position doing repetitive motion for a long time. On a day like that, you may not want any more stress on your body in order to stay healthy.

But if you had a light load that day, got plenty of exercise, ate well, gave your parents and siblings some attention, then you might be able to enjoy a game or show or catching up with what your friends and followers are doing online. It's about looking at the whole picture.

What about when we have friends over? Can we game or watch videos together? Can we check out our Social Media pages?

Do you remember being a little kid and play dates were about compromise? Making sure you and your guest both had a chance to do what you wanted to do, taking turns, working together? Hanging out with friends is still the same now. If you have a friend over it's important to socialize with the person in front of you! There are different ways to do that and gaming together can be social! Sometimes even watching a show together or laughing at a YouTube video together can be social. But when two people sit down next to each other and play separately, you might as well be alone!

It not about whether or not you can use technology in front of a friend, it's about what you are doing with the technology and for how long. The same rules apply about your health and wellness when you have a friend over. Don't sit and stare at a screen for more time than you are moving around. Take frequent breaks so as not to cause repetitive stress injuries, give the person you are with plenty of face-to-face attention, and make sure both people are engaged in what you are doing.

38

Rather than focusing on screen time, think of the activity as a creative outlet where they are working together and having fun. As long as everyone has a say in how their image will be used, this can be a great experience.

The 3 Golden Rules

I want to take this opportunity to emphasize a point I was trying to make in the last chapter. I believe you don't need a whole bunch of "dos and don't" about screen time, cell phone use, social media, etc. If you are just willing to follow the three Golden Rules:

1.   You do not disobey a direct order

2.   You do not lie

3.   You are never disrespectful

By following these three rules, you set yourself up for success every time. All you have to do is remember that you are in the driver's seat of your own destiny.

Let's look at an example:

SIMPLE right?

But what happens...

If after the 15 minutes when it's time to leave, the child NOW remembers she needs to brush her teeth and put on her shoes...

Answer: SHE'S TOAST!

Which two rules did she break?

Yep. **Disobeying a direct order AND she LIED!** She wasn't ready to leave.

This is where most of you run into problems with your parents or guardians. There's a lot to do as a parent, having to ask you over and over again... well, it's just plain FRUSTRATING! But there's a flip side to this... it's not fair when you are in the middle of a game, show, project, book, etc. and an adult comes in without warning and tells you to stop what you are doing and move on to something else. That can be just as frustrating for you! So what to do? It's time to start managing your time better.

There is a simple formula to avoid battles related to screen time and to ensure you won't be shouting:

Lori's secret formula to extinguish screen time battles:

FIRST: Find out how much time you have to do what you want before you start.

SECOND: Decide if you have enough time to do what you want and can stop when time is up. Otherwise, don't start something you are not going to be able to finish or come back to later.

What you may be thinking...

Well then, it may NOT be the right show, game, social media, app, etc. for you to use right now! You may want to try a two week fast (no access at all) from a particular game, social media site or app to help you reset and see if when you return, you are able to set boundaries and stick to them.

Dear Mrs. Getz,

My name is **Leon** and I love GTA (Grand Theft Auto). I know it's rated "M" but I'm not affected by the violence and stuff at all. But I do have a hard time getting off the game at night. Last night I got caught playing in the middle of the night by my dad and he says I can NEVER play GTA again! My mom thinks the reason I am so grumpy in the mornings is because of the game. It's not, I swear! How do I get them to give me back my game?

Sincerely,

Leon (7th grader)

Dear Mrs. Getz,

I'm kinda a social media super star! My fans love to keep up to date on everything going on in my life. I have more than 30,000 followers on Instgram and I don't even know how many subscribers on YouTube. My fans depend on me. I always know what's trending and I'm even a bit of a trend setter. It's exhausting! I am also starting to notice that I can't stop myself from refreshing my apps constantly to see new comments and likes and find out if I have more followers.

I know it's affecting my school work and also my relationship with my friends. But I just can't stop myself! Help!

Tifini (8th grader)

I received these letters last year from students and asked if I could publish them. Leon and Tifini agreed (thanks, guys).

These are common questions and here is what I have to say on the subject: Gaming and social media are great fun. I enjoy it myself. But when gaming and social media become an obsession, you need to take a hard look whether you control the technology or the technology is controlling you. Take a look at the Review Section to see who or what is in control of your digital life.

Section IV Review

Dr. Kimberly S. Young[1] created a questionnaire to help young people determine if in fact they are addicted to gaming, social media, texting etc. Answer the questions below as honestly as possible. If you answer "yes" to 5 out of 8 questions you may need to look for some serious help. Talk to your parents about your results to decide the best course of action for you.

Are you preoccupied with using the Internet? Do you think about your previous or future online activity?

☐ Yes   ☐ No

Do you have the need to be online longer to be satisfied?

☐ Yes   ☐ No

Have you made repeated but unsuccessful attempts to cut back, stop or control your Internet use?

☐ Yes   ☐ No

Do you become moody, restless, irritable or depressed when you stop or decrease your Internet use?

☐ Yes   ☐ No

Is your time spent online longer than what you originally planned?

☐ Yes   ☐ No

Did your online use negatively affect a significant relationship (including parents and friends), or school?

☐ Yes   ☐ No

Do you conceal the extent of your Internet usage from your therapist, family or others?

☐ Yes   ☐ No

Does the Internet serve as an escape from problems or relief from a bad mood?

☐ Yes   ☐ No

---

1   NetAddiction. "Dr. Kimberly Young Internet Addiction." NetAddiction. n.d. Web. 19 May 2016. <http://netaddiction.com/kimberly-young/>

Most people are not addicted to gaming, social media, texting, and creating or watching videos. Most people have just developed some bad habits. Can you identify some bad habits people have with technology? Add a star to any bad habits that affect you personally.

Listing YouTube as a bad habit is not what I mean. YouTube isn't a habit, but watching YouTube when you are supposed to being doing homework... now that's a bad habit.

How can you break bad technology habits? *For example; Watching YouTube while doing homework can be resolved by installing a distraction blocker like Stay Focused or Self-Control App to your computer, tablet or mobile device so you can block YouTube for a short period of time while trying to study (These are not controlled by parents but rather you turn them on when you need a little help staying on track).*

FOMO – It's FO-Real!

According to Rebecca Hiscott, reporter for Mashable[2] , there are eight ways technology has rewired our brains. Everything from dreaming in color to phantom vibration syndrome (thinking your phone is vibrating even when it's not). I definitely recommend reading the whole article but for now I want to discuss her view on FOMO (Fear of Missing Out).

FOMO is a real thing but it's not a new thing. Teenagers have experienced FOMO Forever (even your parents and grandparents experienced this feeling when they were young)! The difference today is the immediate notice when you have not been included in something, which makes you want to stay connected even more, so it doesn't happen again.

For example, you may have plans with your best friend on a Saturday night. You are having a great time UNTIL you check Instagram and see there is a party going on and YOU were not invited. If there wasn't the constant, ever-present commentary of everybody's life at your fingertips you would have enjoyed your quiet Saturday night with your best friend (and maybe not have found out about the party until school on Monday).

So what to do about FOMO? Honestly, there is no good answer here. It's gonna sting when you are not included, no matter what I say or advice I give. I wish I could say, "just grow a thicker skin, ignore it, do something more fun!" But those phrases don't help when you are in the middle of a FOMO meltdown.

So I can only say this- if you are on the OTHER END- meaning you are the person having the party or attending the party, maybe don't publicly post everything you are doing that Saturday night. DM or text the pictures to the people you are with. Be considerate and remember how it feels to be on the other end of exclusion.

2   Hiscott, Rebecca. "8 Ways Tech Has Completely Rewired Our Brains." Mashable. 14 Mar. 2014. Web. 19 May 2016. <http://mashable.com/2014/03/14/tech-brains-neuroplasticity/>

You're Saying She Hates My Guts?
Digital Drama vs. Cyber-bullying

Digital Drama and FOMO often go hand in hand. Digital drama refers to the hurt feelings, confrontations, rumors, and mean spirited actions that are directly related to online actions. When you see a post about someone throwing a party and you weren't invited, there are most definitely hurt feelings and often spurs digital drama. When someone texts you a mean comment or makes fun of something you posted (one time), these too will cause a whole lot of drama!

But digital drama is different than cyber-bullying. Cyber-bullying is the most egregious form of targeting a specific individual over and over again without provocation and with intent to cause a great deal of harm and stress for the person.

Teens don't always mean to cause digital drama. There is something known as an "oops" moment, where you may have reacted too quickly to something, or thought it was a joke but the person targeted didn't find it funny. **When it's in the heat of the moment, your limbic system takes over and you act too fast. What you really needed in that moment was a pause button.** It's one of the big differences between drama and bullying. The other big difference with digital drama is that it happens once, not over and over and over again.

Digital Drama may also include:

We see a lot more digital drama than cyber-bullying. That doesn't make it any better or less painful but the distinction is important.

Digital Drama is the day-to-day nonsense where someone makes a rude comment one time, thinking it's funny but it hurts someone else. It's the mean spirited text that wasn't thought out. It's the over-sharing that goes viral and is now embarrassing. It can even occur without words... when you sit anxiously awaiting a response that doesn't come and you obsess over why! The drama is a bit easier to get away from. Turn off your devices, don't check and recheck and wait until the next day when you can confront the individual causing you grief.

Cyber-bullying is much more pervasive (affects every part of your life).

I don't tell too many stories about myself, but I think this one is important...

When I was a teenager there was a girl that made my life miserable! She started rumors about me, she would tell my friends if they talked to me she would make them miserable too; she would physically intimidate me, constantly crank call me, and even destroyed property and placed it my backpack so I would be blamed.

Every day I would go home and tell my mom about what she was doing to me. I felt alone. I had no one to sit with at lunch. I would hide in a teacher's classroom, just to avoid being near her. I was very sad. But my mom wasn't helpful! She kept telling me that this girl was jealous and insecure. I knew she was wrong. "What did she have to be jealous or insecure about? She controls EVERYTHING," I would shout at my mother.

All these years later, I now know the truth… my mom WAS wrong!

Yes, it's possible when people are causing you drama or bullying you it may be because they are jealous or insecure, or it may be that they have terrible things going on in their own lives, or their parents are bullies so they think their behavior is normal, or… they just don't like you!

The last reason was why my bully was targeting me! She just didn't like me; and I can't imagine my mom saying, I'm sorry sweetheart, she is doing this because she HATES YOUR GUTS!

I wish she had said that to me. It would have made things a little easier for me to understand. If I knew there was nothing I could do to make her like me, maybe I would have spent less time trying to make her not feel jealous or insecure. I wasted so much time trying to convince our mutual friends that I was RIGHT and she was hateful. But it never worked. My friends were either too scared to stand up for me OR they just didn't see things the way I did. And I believe the latter was the truth in my situation. My bully was not their bully; she was their friend. They might have been a little afraid of getting involved too. As long as they were on her good side, they were safe.

I know in the movies the victim always gets justice, but that's not real life. You can't control what other people do, you can only control your reaction.

Did I get revenge? Kinda - but not the kind you see in the movies. **I got happy!** HOW? You ask…

I surrounded myself with a new group of friends that really cared about me. I stopped talking about her (that only gives the bully control when you constantly talk about him/her). I would make plans with other people on the weekends so I had fun things to do to keep me occupied. I got a lot of hugs from my mom. And I talked to my school counselor to get advice.

Ignoring doesn't work! But rather I started to learn that when I felt good about myself, I cared less about what she thought. I'll be honest- it wasn't a quick fix. I had to work on my self-esteem every day. And my new group of friends gave me the confidence to move forward. Once I got over the fact that I wanted everyone to hate her as much as I did, I was able to look forward at what I did have. You can't do it alone. You need a support system.

Today's Cyber-bullying and digital drama is even MORE difficult than what I faced as a teen because it's everywhere and you can't get away from it. It follows you and everyone seems to know about it (even kids at other schools due to the viral nature of the net). So how do YOU take control?

 Stop – do not interact with the bully. By choosing not to engage online, the victim takes control of the situation. Not engaging is very different than ignoring! Ignoring means that you pretend like it's not happening. It is happening, and it's time to learn how to stand up and take control. Body language is vitally important when you stands up for yourself, and this cannot be done in a chat room or via text message. The bully needs to see that the victim is unwilling to accept the harassment. Whether the victim chooses to walk away with confidence, surround him or herself with good friends or look the bully in the eye, your body language and tone of voice make all the difference. By trying to defend yourself online, the victim usually gets caught in a web of name calling and threats that only make the situation worse. When the victim CHOOSES to stop interacting, shuts it off, and reaches out to parents, a trusted adult or other close friends, they begin to rebuild self-esteem rather than go on a mission to locate every hateful thing ever said to or about them.

If you are the victim, you may not feel comfortable confronting the bully face-to-face. That's okay. Ask for help! Find a trusted adult who can guide you through focusing on rebuilding your self-esteem and finding a support system.

One of the reasons a lot of teens tell me that they don't want their parents involved is because sometimes parents can make it worse. They might call the school, or the bully's parents, or contact the bully directly. YIKES! It's important that when you tell your parents about what is going on, you also tell them what you need!

For some parents, it is tempting to expend energy trying to "get the bully that hurt their child" and sometimes, when the bullying happens anonymously, adults will spend time and even money trying to expose the true culprit. But that may or may not help the victim in the end.

What if you can't figure out who the online bully is? OR worse, what if you find out it was someone you do know and thought was your friend? What if when the bully is confronted, they deny it and it's hard to prove?

I'm not saying that bullies should get away with appalling behavior. I think people who bully others are GROSS! And when they do it in an anonymous way I think they are cowards!

But I can't promise you justice. I wish I could! So the best thing to do is STOP. Stop looking, stop searching for it, stop engaging and tell your friends you don't want to hear about it. Every time you look or engage you feel it all over again. But when you stop, you give yourself a break and you can begin to heal.

Block – stop the user from sending any more messages. Most systems have a way to block a user, account or phone number. If the bullying is happening anonymously, then shut down YOUR ACCOUNT on the application being used to transmit the messages. If the bullying becomes overwhelming, the victim may even want to change their cell phone number, e-mail, IM, or social networking accounts and start over again with a smaller group of friends they know they can trust.

Report - print out the entire conversation and tell someone! Document the situation so you feel some control but then hand it off to a trusted adult! When you report to a trusted adult it's important to tell them what you hope to accomplish and what you need from them.

Most websites, including gaming sites, social networking, or anywhere you can interact with other users, have a way to report abuse. That should be the first reporting you do with the help of a trusted adult. Why get an adult involved? You might ask... because remember that frontal lobe issue? Yeah- in the heat of the moment you are NOT going to make great decisions and may end up making things worse.

CAUTION Depending on the site and the degree of bullying, the system may do everything from warning the culprit, to shutting down an account, or contacting law enforcement. Different states have different laws about Cyber-bullying, however, if you are being harassed or threatened online, if someone is making physical threats, or your scared to go to school or the activity where the bullying is happening, contact local law enforcement immediately! No one has the right to make you feel unsafe!

Bystanders play a major role in how far the bullying will go. When bystanders choose to stand by the victim or even let the bully know they do not condone the behavior, the victim feels supported. Bystanders often feel helpless because they are not aware of their options when they see another person being bullied. Some bystanders feel it is not their place to get involved if they are not directly targeted, the target is not a close friend, they are not participating in the bullying, or there may be consequences for them if they get involved.

If you are a bystander you need to know you have three options:

1. **Stand up** to the bully: Let the bully know their behavior is unacceptable and will not be tolerated (this is a good option if you are very confident in your own personal relationships, or have a direct and close relationship with the bully and therefore your separation from the bully may cause the bully to feel unsupported and alone in their efforts).

2. **Stand by** the victim (either publicly or privately): Letting the victim know they are supported and have people who care about them is vitally important! When a victim feels supported, it can help boost their self-esteem so they can stand up for themselves.

3. **Stand tall**: Tell an adult. Let a trusted adult know what is going on. Tell them the facts! Talk about it together how you might be able to support the victim or if it's necessary take it to the right authorities.

It's never a bad idea to practice how you will deal with a bullying situation. Maybe even do some role-playing with an adult so you know how to react if you ever find yourself in a sticky situation.

Section V Review

Have you ever caused digital drama or been a cyber-bully? What did you do and why did you do it?

Have you ever been a victim of digital drama or cyber-bullying? What happened and how did you respond?

Have you ever been a bystander of digital drama or cyber-bullying? What happened and how did you respond?

Are You a Healthy Person?

Do you consider yourself a healthy person? Is your body healthy? Do you get plenty of exercise? Sleep well? Have strong concentration and learning habits? Do you try to eat well? Do you have healthy relationships with your friends and family?

You may not have answered YES to all of these questions and that's okay. We want to STRIVE to be the best we can be. You don't have to be perfect, just aware! So I need to give you some more facts about health and wellness as it pertains to technology.

So far we have discussed ergonomic health (screen time and stress on your body), social emotional health (FOMO, Digital Drama and Cyber-bullying) and even relationship health (understanding the guidelines of online relationships and spending plenty of face-to-face time with people you care about). Now let's focus a little more on your physical and mental well-being.

There is a lot to discuss with regard to your physical health and it starts with sleep. It's an important topic with some big issues, but some simple solutions.

We know how important sleep is. It improves memory[3], spurs creativity, improves athletic performance, improves attention, increases metabolism (helps with weight management), lowers stress, and decreases depression. Basically, when you get a good night sleep, you are at your best!

But why are so many of us not sleeping well these days? It may have something to do with our technology.

There are a few reasons technology may be affecting sleep:

1. **The light from the devices causes a reduction in melatonin[4]**, the hormone that helps you fall asleep and stay asleep. The light acts as a cue to the brain telling the brain it is daytime instead of nighttime. There are now several devices that allow you to turn on the "night vision" option that reduces the light that negatively affects sleep. We should use it IF we need to read on a device before bed. But if we don't need it before bed, it's better not to use it at all. Here's why... reason #2...

2. **You don't turn it off.** In the same study, participants who read a paper book before bed found it easier to turn off the lights at the designated 10 p.m. time and go to sleep. Not only did they fall asleep faster, but they had fewer problems putting down the book. Participants in the study using devices, had a VERY HARD time logging off. It is always, one more text, one more game, one more episode of your favorite TV show and soon it's 2 a.m. and you are still WIDE AWAKE !

Many teens tell me the reason they use technology at bedtime is because they CAN'T fall asleep so it gives them something to do. Guess what? You are now stuck in a vicious cycle! The technology is keeping you awake so you continue to use it because you are awake! Then,

---

3   Health.com. "11 Surprising Health Benefits of Sleep." Health.com. 19 May 2016. Web. 19 May 2016. <http://www.health.com/health/gallery/0,,20459221,00.html>
4   http://www.scientificamerican.com/article/q-a-why-is-blue-light-before-bedtime-bad-for-sleep/

there is reason #3; EMFs disrupt sleep.

3. **EMFs. What are they? Electro Magnetic Field.** EMFs are a type of energy that is emitted by all electronics (anything that plugs into a wall). EMFs result in a form of non-ionized radiation. I know – radiation is a scary word - but this is a different type of radiation than what comes out of an X-Ray machine or a nuclear plant. We are surrounded by these EMFs all day long. Here's the problem though, in large doses and in close proximity, these EMFs can penetrate the brain and cause activity (studies are still being done to better understand the long term effects). That means if you are sleeping next to your device, your brain is active all night long! Now that's not restful sleep.

High levels of EMF exposure have been linked to memory loss, depression, brain fog, fatigue, weight gain and muscle aches[5]. It's not a guarantee that if you use a cell phone you will suffer these symptoms but why not mitigate (reduce) your risks?

Although all electronics, including lamps, clocks, and speakers, emit EMFs we don't tend to carry them around with us all day long or sleep with them under our pillows! We save that behavior for our cell phone, wearable technology and other mobile devices. The more distance we can put between our electronics and our heads, the better off we will be.

Is it possible that my wearable technology is keeping me awake?

According to the FCC website[6], all consumer electronics such as cell phones are tested to ensure their safety. However, even the FCC cannot deny that we still don't know enough and mitigation of risk is just prudent (a good idea). Using a wired ear piece is better than putting your phone to your head.

But my cell phone is my alarm clock.

Getting an old school alarm clock is really best but if you NEED to use your cell phone as an alarm clock, can you at least stop using it 45 minutes before bed, put it on Airplane Mode and set it up across the room?

It's not about giving up technology, it's about taking the current information we have and making the best decisions possible. All of these devices and their affects on humans are still relatively NEW. It means we are a generation of guinea pigs.

I don't keep my phone in my pocket, tucked into my shirt or in my hand if I'm not using it. There just isn't a reason for me to possibly put my health at risk if I can avoid issues by making some small changes.

There is still A LOT we don't know about health risks related to all of the new technology, so let's not go overboard and throw the devices in the trash, but using common sense can mitigate our risks. For all these reasons I say, get the technology out of your room. You'll sleep better, won't stay up so late, and you can rest easy knowing you are doing everything possible to be healthy

5   N.a. "FAQs about EMFs." Emfcenter.com. 30 Jun. 2010. Web. 19 May 2016. <http://www.emfcenter.com/emffaqs.htm>

6   Federal Communications Commission. "Radio Frequency Safety." Federal Communications Commission. 2 Mar. 2011. Web. 16 Sept. 2016. <https://www.fcc.gov/general/radio-frequency-safety-0>

and well (not to mention you'll be less likely to send a crude message or inappropriate post; people do the silliest things when they are tired).

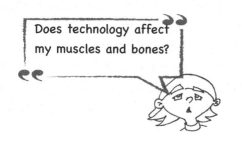

Does technology affect my muscles and bones?

The way you use technology definitely has an effect on your whole body!

According to Ergonomics specialist, Jim Taylour, our posture is affected by how we sit at a computer or gaming console and use mobile devices. Every time we look down to read our phones we put stress on our neck. In small doses, no problem. In large doses...well you may be cuasing problems with your head, neck, back, wrists, hands and fingers.

Here are a few tips from teens who have struggled with pain due to overuse of technology:

Try holding your phone at eye level.

Sit up straight at the computer with a keyboard and mouse in the correct position and with your feet flat as often as you can. Take frequent breaks and stretch and change positions.

Put it down when you are not using it so your hand isn't constantly in the same position.

My mom tells me that technology related distractions are bad for my brain. What is she talking about?

YES, your developing brain is affected by technology; it can be a big issue but has some simple solutions.

Have you ever started reading something and then you were interrupted? You lose your place and have to backtrack in order to remember what you just read. Or have you ever studied for a test and did well, but three days later you don't remember ANY of the information?

This is all very common and has nothing to do with how smart you are and everything to do with your brain strength.

We can all have stronger brains if we spend time exercising it. Most teens tend to study with their pre-frontal cortex: this is the part of the brain used to take in information and decide what to do with it. You might refer to it as the multitasking part of your brain.

Yes, multitasking is a real thing, but misunderstood. Multitasking is the ability to DO lots of things in rapid succession – meaning one right after another. It's why you think you can DO homework while watching TV.

Homework is such a pain! It takes me FOREVER to get it done. I complain to my parents but they just keep telling me it's because I'm distracted by group texts, watching videos and music. They tell me I can't multitask but I KNOW I can. I do it all the time. I can have 6 different group texts going, watch TV, and making a new iTunes playlist. When I try to just sit and read a book, I can't help but think of all the things I would rather be doing online. It's not my fault! It's just the way my brain works.

But there is a BIG difference between DOING and LEARNING! When you watch TV and DO homework, you are not retaining the information. The information hits the pre-frontal cortex, is applied to the task at hand and then just vanishes from your memory.

When you do well on the test but can't remember the material three days later... that's in part because you are studying with the wrong part of your brain!

You need your hippocampus engaged in order to form and store memories. And the only way to engage your hippocampus is to focus on one thing at a time.

Imagine you are reading a book for social studies and you're also involved in a large group chat or text. Every time your device alerts you of an incoming message, dopamine is released in your brain and that makes you happy. So of course you WANT to see what the message says, and you interrupt yourself, causing a break in the chain of information trying to get to your hippocampus. It's not like you can just pick up where you left off and keep moving forward. It doesn't work like that.

Imagine that information travels through your brain trying to reach the area where long-term memories are stored and can later be retrieved (like for a final exam). Each time you break the chain because you or are interrupted by a text, notification, YouTube Video, a parent walking into the room and asking, "how's it going?" that chain breaks.

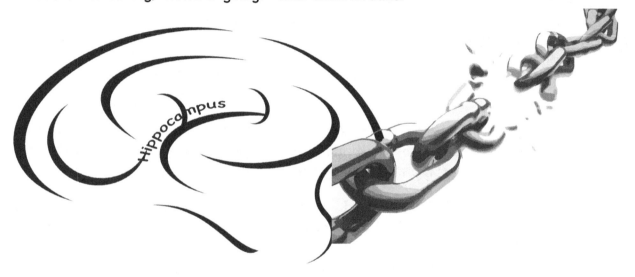

Before you can move to the next link, you have to repair the broken one. That repair takes time and effort, thus making it much more difficult to learn, retain and later retrieve information.

Find a kid in class you think is super smart. Ask him or her how they do homework and study. I bet you that they don't have devices surrounding them that distract them while trying to learn.

So while YES, you absolutely CAN multitask, you most definitely CANNOT learn that way.

There is one caveat (exception) to this...music.

Some research has shown that music can actually help people concentrate. It takes them to a place where they are calm and are able to think along the melody of the music . Rather than the music being a distraction it's like a river on which you can float to learning. However, the music cannot be something you are singing along to the lyrics. Some people find classical or jazz music to be helpful. Some even use video game music to keep them on task!

Try it out. What's the harm? Try doing a certain type of homework one night without any distractions. No TV, YouTube, texts, social media for just the time of a particular assignment. Tell yourself that the moment you finish you can take a break from your work or studies and check in online. There are great applications and plug-ins like StayFocused and Self-Control App that will block distracting websites and applications while on a computer, laptop, tablet or mobile device. Tell your friends you will be offline for 30 minutes. Then turn your mobile devices into Airplane Mode or Do Not Disturb. Dive into your work for just 25-30 minutes and see if you are more productive. I know I always am!

Section VI Review

What are three healthy changes you can make with regard to your technology use?

1. _____

2. _____

3. _____

How can you set yourself up for success when doing homework or studying?

Be An Original

We all love music, movies and software. So if we want people to continue making these things, WE HAVE TO STOP STEALING IT!

Listen, I get it. If you can get it for free why would you pay for it? But it's not fair and it's not legal. Remember the definition of FAIR? It means everyone gets what they need. And when you steal music, movies and software, the creators, the distributors, even the secretaries and the janitorial crew at the company - they don't get what they need - a pay check!

Sometimes teens tell me,

> But the artists make enough money from concerts and merchandise. They're NOT going to miss my $1.29!

Okay, four things to that statement: **First**, if everyone felt the way you did that drop in revenue would be so significant that artist would stop creating.

Second, it's not just the artist who is affected by this. It the sound engineers, the maintenance crews who work in the buildings, the ticket-taker at the movie theater and everyone in between.

Third, its not ethical! You are stealing. Just because you may or may not get caught doesn't mean it's okay to do.

Finally, there's one more issue with piracy. The websites that let you access music, movies and software for free are usually Peer-to-Peer share sites. This means you are accessing someone else's computer to get to the files. That means anything on their computer can be transmitted to yours... including VIRUSES!

It's just not worth it.

Welcome to the HUB

Imagine if your house had a charging station like this. It would live in the kitchen and EVERYONE (including the grown-ups) in the house used it. It's where the phones, tablets and laptops live when they are not in use.

It's not a punishment. It's a reminder that there is a time and a place for everything. Sometimes when we get home from school or work we don't realize we are still holding our devices in our hands. So we do things like have half a conversation with someone in the house, while actively have multiple conversations with friends online.

Many of us feel a PULL to stay connected, but we end up ignoring the person right in front of us. Our devices have become an electronic leash!

The charging station is a reminder for the whole family that when you walk in the house, your priority is your family. I even know a dad who stays in the garage and finishes up working before he walks into his house to see his kids. That way the moment he enters, he feels good about disconnecting from work and ready to connect with his wife and children. The phone goes on the charging station and his family has his attention.

This technology hub has been incredibly helpful in so many ways in my own home. My kids keep the devices there and when they want to use them, they just say, "Mom, I'm gonna text Caitlin, okay?"

And my response is usually "Sure!" As long as we are not about to sit down to dinner, leave the house or start homework. I like to be able to GIVE technology rather than taking it away. When my daughter is done, she simply puts the device back on the HUB.

The devices also live here when we all go to bed. This way they stay out of the bedroom, giving you an opportunity to get a good night sleep, they don't get lost, and in the morning they are fully charged and ready for the day.

Simple and SO Helpful!

To Spy or Not to Spy

There are only a few times in this book where I tell you that you HAVE TO do something. I really want you to come to your own conclusions and make healthy, well-thought out decisions based on facts (looking at the best case, most likely case and worst case scenarios). But this one...well it's just something you NEED to do.

Your parents or guardians NEED access to your online world. That means everything from your passcode to your phone, to a list of every online account and your usernames and passwords. This is not an issue of trust but of PERSONAL SAFETY! Just like you have rules about telling your parents where you are and who you are with, there are a set of safety rules in the digital world too. This rule doesn't just apply to you, but everyone in your house should have at least one person who has access to this information.

"It's not spying if I tell you I'm looking!"

"Why are you spying on me?"

In my house it's not a problem. The adults in the house have access to each other's accounts and to our kids' accounts. My husband and I are totally transparent about our ability to see what our kids are doing online and with whom they are communicating.

Are you wondering if we read ALL of their text messages or track their surfing activity? The answer is sometimes. I completely respect my children's right to privacy. If the bedroom door is closed, I knock first. I don't barge into their bathroom, or put my ear to the door when they have a friend over. Any place my children have an expectation of privacy, they receive that privacy.

But online, remember- there is no expectation of privacy. You gave up the right to CONTROL your information the moment you transmitted it electronically.

But I do understand that there are things you want to talk about with friends where you don't necessarily want your parents hovering. You need to sit down with your parents or guardian and set up a system that works for everyone in the house. If you are transparent about your online life and relationships, your parents won't feel the need to SPY. If mom or dad walks by while you are texting and asks, "who are you texting?" And you respond with, "IT'S NONE OF YOUR BUSINESS!" Your parents are going to spy, and you will cause a whole lot of unnecessary DRAMA in the house.

But, if mom or dad walks by while you are texting and asks, "who are you texting?" And you respond honestly, "Tyler, we are talking about getting together this weekend," your parents are going to be much less likely to feel the need to put spyware on your devices and track your every move.

If it's really private, don't text it, don't tweet it, don't DM it, don't PM it, don't SnapChat it, don't post it, don't comment on it or like it; save the "truly private" for face-to-face. If you think your parents COULD see it, and that would upset or embarrass you, it doesn't belong online!

I can see where my family is at all times. Using apps like Find My Friends lets me see their locations. But I only look when I NEED to look. My family knows that I can see where they are. For me, again, it's a matter of safety. The fact that technology gives me an opportunity to make sure my family is as safe as possible is an advantage I will take! BUT, just because I can look doesn't mean I am tracking my family members at all times.

As parents, our job is to love you and keep you safe, no matter how much you push back. We are not supposed to be your friend, we are your guardian and that's a huge responsibility that can be scary for us sometimes.

You can make this easy, or you can make it difficult on yourself. If you are honest, respectful and understand your frontal lobe is under-developed and you cannot always use reason, logic and impulse control when making decisions, you can have an honest conversation with your parents about what you need from them and they can be honest about what they need from you. Believe it or not, you have more power than you realize. It just requires your willingness to engage in a meaningful conversation with your parents.

Are you freaking out about this section? If so, here is a possible compromise. Write down every account, username, password and passcode on a piece of paper. Get a piggy bank that has no plug at the bottom (so it can't be easily accessed). Put the paper in the piggy bank. That way if your parents need to access the information inside they will need to smash the porcelain piggy, and you will know!

Section VII Review

Where do you fall on the desired privacy scale?

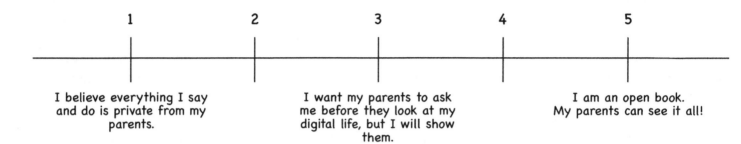

1	2	3	4	5
I believe everything I say and do is private from my parents.		I want my parents to ask me before they look at my digital life, but I will show them.		I am an open book. My parents can see it all!

Now I must ask, WHY? Why did you circle that response? It's important that when you have these types of conversations you think before you speak. Otherwise you end up saying things like, "I don't know, it's just what everyone does these days."

That answer never sits well with parents. So instead, give it some thought. Understand your own feelings about privacy and where your parents or guardians fit in. Remember, as a teen, it's really hard – almost impossible – to imagine anything bad can happen to you. It's just how your brain is wired right now. Instead of focusing on best-case or worst-case scenarios, go to the middle and think about the most-likely case scenario when talking to your parents about privacy.

Where do you fall on the desired privacy scale and why?

Manners Count

You have learned not to chew with your mouth open, not to interrupt when someone is talking, to say please and thank you, to wait your turn, to consider other people's feelings and so on and so on! We understand the rules of society in real life. But do we understand the rules of society online as well?

1. **If you are in a public place and need to take a call, speak softly or find a more private place to talk.** It's distracting to the people around you and strangers really don't need to be all up in your business!

2. Do you remember when you were a little kid and you would get in trouble for interrupting adults while they were talking? The same goes if they are on the phone or in the middle of a text. **Wait until you are seen and remember to say, "excuse me."**

3. **On the flip side... say "excuse me" and walk away before taking a call or sending a text or checking social media.** Whether you are at the dinner table with your family or hanging out with friends, no one likes to feel ignored.

4. **No need to text if you have nothing to say.** At some point you just need to STOP!

5. **Please stop text stalking your friends.** If your best friend doesn't respond right away it's not necessarily because she doesn't like you anymore. You cause drama in your own head wondering why she is not responding. Just turn off your device or do something else. She's probably just busy.

6. **Break the chain.** If someone sends you an email or text that says, "send this to five people or something bad will happen," I promise nothing bad will happen if you don't forward the message. However, if you DO forward the message you are most likely supplying a spammer or hacker with other people's personal information.

7. **Please don't bring your friends into MY bathroom!** I can't believe I even have to say this, but please DO NOT carry your FaceTime conversation into places where your family members have an expectation of privacy.

8. **Play fair and be a good sport.** In the world of gaming, remember we were all new to the game at one point so be kind and a little patient! Teamwork is a great skill so you might as well start learning it now. So play fair, don't spam the chat feature, starting a flame war is lame and can get you kicked off the server and PLEASE... no cheats! Be a good sport and remember it is supposed to fun for everyone.

9. **The law of accepting or rejecting a friend or follow request is tricky.** Ask yourself this: "Why would I allow or disallow this request?" If it's out of spite or vengeance, then you are in the wrong. However, you should only accept people you truly trust! Remember, once they are following you they control everything you post. It's a tricky situation sometimes and a great time to blame your parents. If someone asks you at school why you didn't accept their request, you can tell them that your parents are in charge of that and make the final decision.

10. Are you bilingual? Do you know when to use text lingo and when to use academic English? **Please don't "Hey" your teachers.** We are not your buddies. Use our proper title, greetings and salutations when communicating electronically with adults.

11. Know when to text and when to call. **When texting becomes a conversation, it's time to talk.** Best rule of thumb, if you are not making plans but discussing something personal and you go back and forth three times, pick up the phone. There's another piece to this: you need to know your audience. Your friends might be okay with texting but your grandmother might prefer a phone call. Be sensitive to others and try and think about their needs as well.

12. Know **when to send direct and when to share with many.** Think about whether something is meant for one person or many. Don't publicly post inside jokes, pics or comments that exclude others. "Great party- ken chens!" belongs in a private message or small group text!

13. Ranting too often quickly becomes annoying! **Not everything in life is meant to make you miserable.** Keep life in perspective. There is nothing wrong with offering an opinion when it's asked for, but ranting about every little thing can be seen as obnoxious.

14. If you are supposed to be asleep, most likely your friends should be too. **So be considerate and don't text them after hours.**

15. No one likes a stalker. It's creepy and weird and it can affect YOUR self-esteem and feelings about relationships. **If you find yourself constantly checking in on someone you may need to take a serious break.** Think about your intentions and your health. If you need help ASK a trusted adult.

Final Thoughts

Here's the last thing I want to say. Technology is awesome. Truly awesome. If it weren't for YouTube I wouldn't know how to Whip and Nae nae or change a bike tire. Without Twitter, I wouldn't be able to keep up with all of the interesting things Presidential candidates say during their campaigns. Without SnapChat, I couldn't send my hubby a Valentine photo with hearts for eyes. Without FaceTime, I wouldn't be able to SEE my kids before bed when I am traveling hundreds of miles away. Without my Calendar on my phone, I would never know where to be and when!

Technology can and should make life better, it can enhance relationships, it can bring people together for a common cause, and IT'S FUN. Now that you have a better understanding of how it all works, I hope you feel empowered. Remember, it's your behavior that matters.

Do you want more control in your life? Take it now. From here on, make better choices about the things you share, the people you meet, the comments you make, and your health. You'll quickly see how much more control you have.

Parent/Child Acceptable Use Contract

Child

☐ I agree to tell my parents/trusted adult if someone I do not know contacts me.

☐ I agree to tell my parents/trusted adult if I become aware of or involved in a cyber-bullying situation.

☐ I agree to ask my parents/trusted adult before opening any type of account or downloading any application to my computer, laptop, cell phone, iPod Touch or other personal electronic device.

Both Parent and Child

☐ I agree to keep all personal information private: others and mine. This includes:

_____

_____

☐ I agree that a certain amount of online attention is inappropriate. This includes:

_____

_____

☐ I agree that online communication with strangers is only acceptable when:

_____

_____

☐ I agree that I will share my account information and passwords in the following manner:

_____

_____

☐ I agree that stealing music, videos and software from the Internet is equivalent to shoplifting. I will only download copyrighted material that I have paid for.

☐ I agree that an appropriate amount of screen time is (this is not necessarily a number or even the same each day. See Chapter "That's Not Fair" for more information):

Weekdays: _____

Weekends: _____

☐ I agree the computer, laptop, cell phone, ipod touch and other electronic devices will be used in these areas only:

_____

_____

☐ I agree the computer, laptop, cell phone, ipod touch and other electronic devices will not go to bed with me, rather they will be charged in this location:

_____

_____

Parent

☐ I agree not to over-react if I learn that my child has been contacted by a stranger or becomes aware of or involved in a cyber-bullying situation.

☐ I agree to talk before saying NO to additional technological devices and/or applications.

_____

_____

☐ I agree to do my due diligence to learn about my child's online community the same way I take interest in his/her activities and friendships in the real world.

☐ I agree to find an appropriate balance between monitoring, spying and privacy. This includes:

_____

_____

Resources

Here are a list of other resources that you might find helpful:

Common Sense Media: To learn more about apps, games, social media sites, movies and more. The site rates the content and provides an explanation about how it was rated. You will also find helpful comments from teens about media content.

Acceptable Use Policy: Build an Acceptable Use Policy that makes sense in your household. For a free download visit http://www.lorigetz.com/aup.html.

Teen Line Online: Get help from a professional or ask the advice of another teen. They can help with anything from digital drama to depression. Don't go it alone. If you need help, please reach out. This is a good place to start if you are not comfortable talking to a parent or other trusted adult.

Potential Suicide Reporting: If you are concerned that you might hurt yourself or a friend might cause harm to him or herself, please contact the Suicide Prevention Line immediately. You can call (800) 273-8255 or go online to https://www.suicidepreventionlifeline.org.

National Center for Missing and Exploited Children: If you are concerned that you (or a friend) may be interacting with a predator online please call (800) 843-5678 or go online to http://www.missingkids.org/CyberTipline.

Made in the USA
Columbia, SC
26 September 2020